Eddie a res...

At t s

Daniel Nunn

Raintree

Raintree is an imprint of Capstone Global Library Limited, a company incorporated in England and Wales having its registered office at 7 Pilgrim Street, London, EC4V 6LB – Registered company number: 6695582

www.raintreepublishers.co.uk
myorders@raintreepublishers.co.uk

First published in hardback in 2014
Paperback edition first published in 2015

Edited by Rebecca Rissman, Daniel Nunn, and Catherine Veitch
Designed by Jo Hinton-Malivoire
Original illustrations © Capstone Global Library Ltd 2013
Illustrations by Steve Walker
Picture research by Ruth Blair
Production by Sophia Argyris
Originated by Capstone Global Library Ltd
Printed and bound in China by Leo Paper Products Ltd

ISBN 978 1 406 26311 4 (hardback)
17 16 15 14 13
10 9 8 7 6 5 4 3 2 1

ISBN 978 1 406 26316 9 (paperback)
18 17 16 15 14
10 9 8 7 6 5 4 3 2 1

British Library Cataloguing in Publication Data
A full catalogue record for this book is available from the British Library.

Acknowledgements
We would like to thank the following for permission to reproduce photographs: Corbis pp. 12 (© Walter Lockwood), 17 (© Pete Marovich/ZUMA Press), 20 (© John Lund); Getty Images p. 22 (Chip Simons); Shutterstock pp. 7l (© Nastya22), 7r (© Mark Hayes), 8 (© CreativeNature.nl), 9t (© Steve Snowden), 9b (© Hung Chung Chih), 10 (© Eric Isselee), 11t (© Cosmin Manci), 11b (© Marcel Jancovic), 12 (© Walter Lockwood), 13 (© konstantynov), 14 (© Noam Armonn), 15 (© Ianych), 16 (© Steve Snowden), 18, 19 (© Ljupco Smokovski), 21 (© Hung Chung Chih), 23 (© Kruglov_Orda).

Cover photograph of a clown reproduced with permission of Shutterstock (© Fotocrisis).

Every effort has been made to contact copyright holders of any material reproduced in this book. Any omissions will be rectified in subsequent printings if notice is given to the publisher.

Contents

Meet Eddie and Ellie

This is Eddie the Elephant.

And this is Ellie the Elephant.

Sometimes, Eddie and Ellie can't stop arguing.

Opposites

Eddie and Ellie like opposite things.

Opposites are completely different from each other.

Eddie only likes **COLD** drinks.
But Ellie only likes **HOT** drinks!

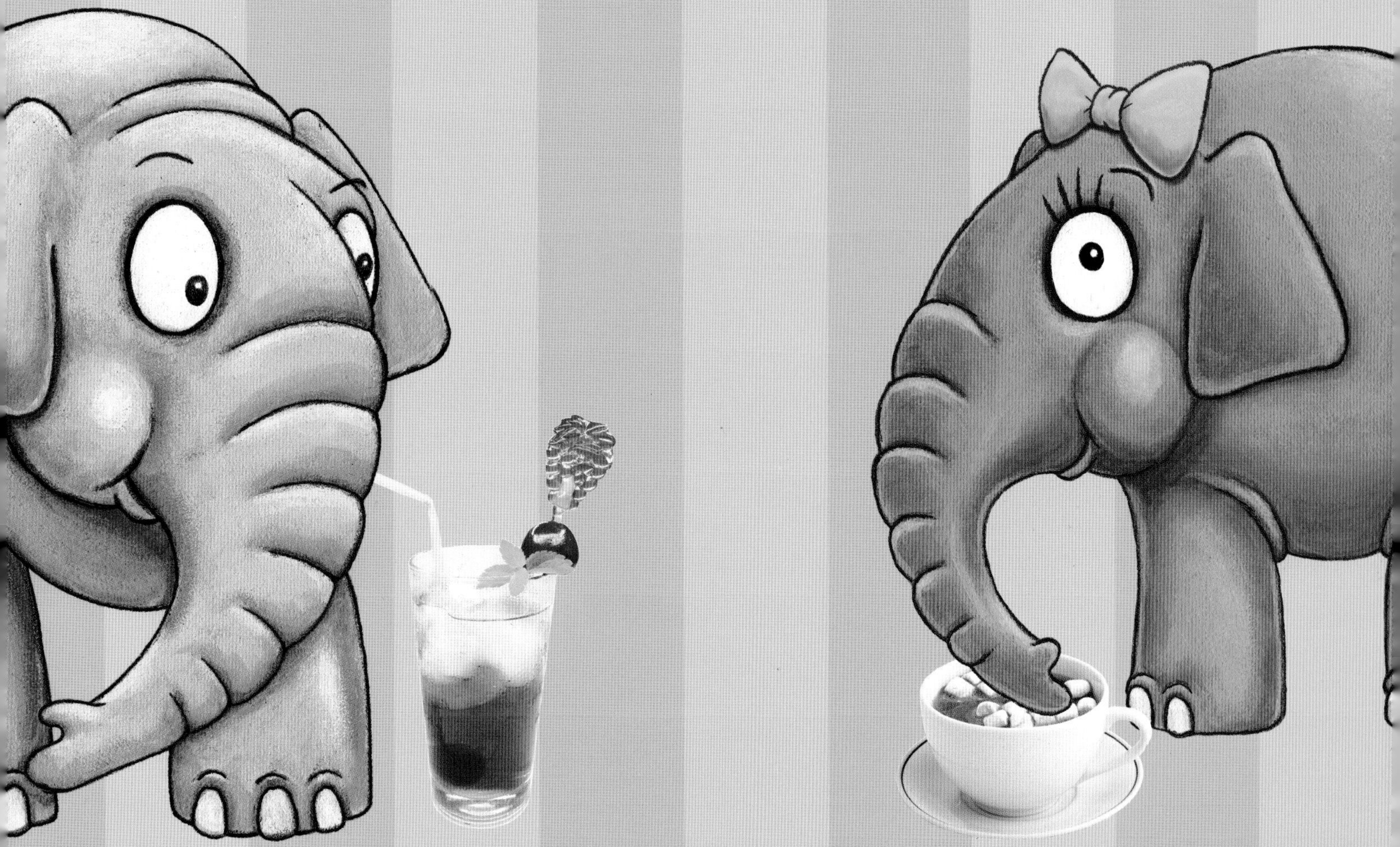

My goodness, what a picky
pair of elephants!

A visit to the circus

Today, Eddie and Ellie are going to the circus.

Clowns, acrobats, trapeze artists, and even animals sometimes perform in a circus.

Big and small

Eddie likes big animals at the circus.

Horses are **BIG**.

Ellie likes small animals at the circus.

Fleas are **SMALL**.

Loud and quiet

Eddie likes loud things at the circus.

This cannon is **LOUD**.

Ellie likes quiet things at the circus.

These mime artists are **QUIET**.

Sad and happy

Eddie likes clowns with sad faces.

This clown has a **SAD** face!

Ellie likes clowns with happy faces.
This clown has a **HAPPY** face.

Curly and straight

Eddie likes clowns with curly hair.

This clown has **CURLY** hair.

Ellie likes clowns with straight hair.
This clown has **STRAIGHT** hair.

Many and a few

Eddie likes jugglers who juggle many things.

This juggler is juggling **MANY** things.

Ellie likes jugglers who juggle a few things.

This juggler is juggling **A FEW** things.

High and low

Eddie likes trapeze artists
who swing way up **HIGH**.
Eeeeek!

Ellie likes contortionists who can bend down **LOW**.

Can you work it out?

Eddie likes to see **FAST** tricks at the circus.

Do you think Ellie likes to see **FAST** tricks, or **SLOW** tricks at the circus?

Opposites quiz

How many of these words do you know the opposites for?

bad **light** **rough**

Answers

Answer to question on page 23

Ellie likes clowns that do slow tricks.

Answers to quiz

The opposite of bad is good.

The opposite of light is dark.

The opposite of rough is smooth.